"Descending Angels"

"Descending Angels"

RICHARD BURSON

WESTBOW
PRESS®
A DIVISION OF THOMAS NELSON
& ZONDERVAN

WestBow Press books may be ordered through booksellers or by contacting:

WestBow Press
A Division of Thomas Nelson & Zondervan
1663 Liberty Drive
Bloomington, IN 47403
www.westbowpress.com
1 (866) 928-1240

All quoted passages of scripture comes from
THE HOLY BIBLE, NEW INTERNATIONAL VERSION®,
NIV® Copyright © 1973, 1978, 1984, 2011 by Biblica, Inc.®
Used by permission. All rights reserved worldwide.

ISBN: 978-1-5127-6370-6 (sc)
ISBN: 978-1-5127-6371-3 (hc)
ISBN: 978-1-5127-6369-0 (e)

Library of Congress Control Number: 2016918539

Print information available on the last page.

WestBow Press rev. date: 11/29/2016

The Heavens opened up and the Angels descended.
Are not all angels ministering spirits sent to
serve those who will inherit salvation?
—Hebrews 1:14

Keep on loving each other as brothers. Do not
forget to entertain strangers for by doing so some
people have entertained angels without knowing it.
—Hebrews 13:1–2

The angel of the Lord encamps around those
who fear him, and he delivers them.
—Psalm 34:7

CONTENTS

This book is dedicated to Jesus, the Christ without whom I would not have salvation or the promise of the angels escorting me into heaven when I die.

It is also dedicated to the love of my life and the one who led me to the foot of the cross, my lovely wife, Josie. She spent countless hours sitting alone on the couch as I plunked away at the computer trying to put my thoughts on paper.

I dedicate this book as well to my children, who are the encouragers in my life. They encouraged me to press on even in the most difficult times. I love you, Susan, Rick, and Rose.

To the hospice team I loved. They taught me so much about the dying and how to care for them.

To the patients and their families I have worked with. They were an inspiration to me and my faith as they faced the valley that no one returns from.

It is also dedicated to my pastor, mentor, friend, and the greatest influence in the ministry God gave to me, Pastor Doyle Collins.

ACKNOWLEDGMENTS

I thank the following people without whose help and contributions I would not have been able to write this book.

Donna Keib, Kovacs Ice Drilling, and Coring Equipment for their generous financial contributions toward the completion of this book.

Larry and Cheryl Young for their encouragement, the great work Larry did to help me develop a workable outline with which to get started and providing an apartment at no charge where I could work with little distraction.

Frank McNeil, my friend and fellow pastor who challenged my theology and kept me true to mine.

Debbie Snell, a fantastic person, hospice nurse, and hospice director.

Dr. Paige Patterson, president of Southwestern Seminary, Fort Worth, Texas, whose example to me has challenged and encouraged me in ministry for over thirty-five years.

INTRODUCTION

While I was serving as a hospice chaplain and a fire chaplain in Oregon, I spent much of my time with those who were dying or with the families of those who had died. As I looked at what was going on around me, I realized that more often than not, I had a different worldview than many did. Many of those I worked with believed death was the end of all things.

I held then and hold now the worldview that death is not the end. It is a passageway for us to move from the physical world to the spiritual, supernatural world that lies beyond the door we call death.

I recently read an article on the Internet that described very well the process a dying person goes through as he or she approaches death and how death ultimately wins. While the article's author's view of the dying process was correct, what struck me was that there was no hope given for more than just dying. He wrote, "We all die and that is the end."

This book will tell a different story. It has a very different ending than that article. I will offer evidence that dying is not the end; my evidence comes from God in the form of Jesus Christ and His death on the cross at Calvary. I have seen the tragedy, hopelessness, and pain of those who have died without hope.

I hope to put hope in the hands of those who are looking for it—something they can look at and hold in their hands—hope for their loved ones beyond death and knowledge they are not in a hopeless dark canyon or a valley by themselves. My hope is this book will be a beacon of light in a time of darkness and concern for them.

I hope some will carry this good news into the future when they will need some light in the darkness, or perhaps it will be something they can share with others who may be going through the same valley of darkness they have been through.

I wrote this book to offer hope to those who are dying and the loved ones who are beside them as they traverse this valley we all must face sometime. There are no trails leading from this valley; we will all walk through it.

Names and locations have been changed to protect the privacy of the families I have served and worked with.

I intend this book to be solace for those in times of great tragedy and in need of hope to get them through those dark times. I hope this book will help those with a finite worldview to have an eternal worldview.

I want to help people change their views on death and dying, to view death not as the end, a dark hopeless place, but as just the next step of many yet to come in eternity.

CHAPTER 1

The Smiling Angel on the Shelf

I love to tell the story of the smiling angel on the shelf. It comes from my experiences as a hospice chaplain. I was called to the hospital to visit a dying woman. I had visited with her a few times in her home before she was admitted to the hospital.

The hospital had a respite room in which the families of hospice patients could wait for the deaths of their loved ones. It contained a large couch, a chair that folded out into a bed, a coffee table, a refrigerator, games, books, and newspapers. The hospital often provided snacks for the families. The hospital staff and personnel were a blessing to the families as they waited in this room for their loved ones to die.

As I entered Mary's room, she greeted me with a great big smile. She always had a smile for me regardless of the amount of pain she was in. I walked to the side of her bed and sat on a chair the family always had there for me.

The hospice nurse had told me Mary didn't have much time left. Her organs had been shutting down over the last few days. I could see purple around her mouth, and her fingertips were blue. Her skin was an off-yellow, another indication it would not be long before she drew her last breath.

Soon, Mary would be escorted into the presence of Jesus by the angels sent to her by God in this moment of glory. One of His loved ones was coming home to be with Him and her loved ones who had gone home before her.

The look on Mary's face let me know she was relaxed at the thought of her impending death. She spoke to me and pointed at something on a shelf near the TV. I bent in to hear what she was saying.

"Pastor, do you see what I see?"

What was she looking at in her final moments of life on earth? What had made her so relaxed?

"Pastor, there's an angel on the TV shelf, and it's smiling at me."

Oh what a blessing and glory to God for His angels who embrace those dying and escort them into the presence of Jesus.

But that raises questions. Who are these angels? Where are they from? What's their origin? Are there any resources we can look at that will tell us about these angels? Simply put, angels are a gift from God to minister to His children who are dying so they will know they won't face death alone or walk through the valley of death by themselves.

Look at what God's Word tells us: "Are not all angels ministering spirits sent to serve those who will inherit salvation?" (Hebrews 1:14).

Death is the transition from the physical world to a spiritual, supernatural world. I like to explain it to the family and to the dying this way. When a baby is created in the womb of a woman, as it grows and develops, the baby finds it has a very comfortable, safe place there. It hears its mother's heartbeat and breathing and feels her warmth. It's a very peaceful, comfortable world for the baby.

Then something begins to happen to the mother's body. It tells her it's time for the baby to be born.

The mother's body creates certain enzymes, and the womb begins to contract. The baby starts wondering what's happening to its world, and it fights to stay in its safe, secure world. But no matter how much it fights the contractions, the baby loses the battle. The birthing process begins. The baby is pushed out of the womb down a dark tube and is born into this great, big world.

This world is stained with sin and is not without its problems, but compared to being in the womb, it's a world beyond the baby's wildest imagination. Even as the umbilical cord is cut, the baby is amazed and would not return to its other world even if it could.

For us, death is what cuts the umbilical cord that holds us to the things of this world. We were designed by God to love life and seek to stay alive as long as possible; that's why we fight so hard to stay alive.

No matter our circumstances or state of health, we fight death. We don't want to die. We don't want to face death. Death is our enemy, and we want to live. Yet beyond the door of death is a world that God's Word describes this way: "What no eye has seen, what no ear has heard, and what no human mind has conceived the things God has prepared for those who love him" (1 Corinthians 2:9).

One of my spiritual heroes is the evangelist D. L. Moody. After having been given up for dead, Moody revived and said God had permitted him to see beyond the thin veil separating the seen from the unseen world. He said he had been "within the gates, and beyond the portals" and had caught a glimpse of familiar faces of those he had "loved long since and lost awhile." He wrote,

> Someday you will read in the paper that D. L. Moody of East Northfield is dead. Don't believe a word of it. At that moment, I shall be more alive than I am now. I shall have gone up higher, that is all. Out of this old clay tenement into a house that is immortal, a body that death cannot touch, that sin cannot taint, and a body fashioned like unto his glorious body.[1]

Charles Spurgeon, the great Baptist preacher, spoke of the glory that attends the death of the children of God.

> If I may die as I have seen some die, I court the grand occasion. I would not wish to

> escape death by some by-road if I may sing
> as they sang. If I may have such hosannas
> and alleluias beaming in my eyes as I have
> and seen and heard from them, it were a
> blessed thing to die.[2]

That is the world beyond death. Death is the enemy, but in Christ, there is eternal life.

In his book *Angels,* Billy Graham told the story of being in London and watching as Queen Elizabeth returned from a trip overseas. He said there were "great crowds, parades of dignitaries, crack troops, and marching bands."[3] He saw all the splendor for a queen returning from a trip. He said that was nothing compared to the homecoming of the believer who has said good-bye to all the suffering of this life and has been immediately surrounded by angels who carry him up to the glorious welcome awaiting them in heaven.

The Word of God tells us the angels rejoice when a soul is saved. Oh what will it be like when children of God come home to be with Him and the angels and their loved ones permanently? What a celebration that will be when we enter through the gates of glory into heaven.

God made us a promise.

> At his gate was laid a beggar named Lazarus, covered with sores and longing to eat what fell from the rich man's table. Even the dogs came and licked his sores. The time came when the beggar died and the angels carried him to Abraham's side. The rich man also died and was buried. (Luke 16:20-22)

Notice what Hebrews 1:14 says: "Are not all angels ministering spirits sent to serve those who will inherit salvation?" God's promise here tells us that angels are with us and will carry us to paradise.

In *Angels*, Billy Graham explained why we will be carried to paradise by the angels following our deaths.

> Death is robbed of much of its terror for the true believer, but we shall need God's protection as we take the last journey. At the moment of death, the spirit departs from the body and moves through the atmosphere. But the Scriptures teach us that the Devil lurks there.

He is "the ruler of the kingdom of the air," (Eph. 2:2. NIV)

If the eyes of our understanding were opened, we would probably see the air filled with demons, the enemies of Christ. If Satan could hinder the angel of Daniel for three weeks on his mission to earth, we can imagine the opposition the Christian may encounter at death.

But Christ on Calvary cleared a road through Satan's kingdom. When Christ came to earth, He had to pass through the devil's territory and open up a beachhead here. That is one reason He was accompanied by a host of angels when he came (Lk 2:8–14 NIV). This is also why the angels will accompany Him when He comes again (Matt. 16:27 NIV).

Until then, the moment of death is still Satan's final opportunity to attack the true believer, but God has sent His angels to guard us at that time.

In telling the story in Luke 16, Jesus says that the beggar was "carried by the angels."

He was not only escorted; he was carried. What an experience that must have been for Lazarus! He had lain begging at the

gate of the rich man until his death, but
suddenly he found himself carried by the
mighty angels of God![4]

I believe Billy Graham said, "Just because we approach death, that doesn't void the promises of God."

Angels are the ministers of God that take us to where Jesus is. In a future date only God knows, Jesus will return and our spirits will reunite with our bodies, which will have gone to graves. But when we die, angels come and take us into the presence of Jesus.

The apostle Paul wrote, "We are confident, I say, and would prefer to be away from the body and at home with the Lord" (2 Corinthians 5:8).

Death is the preparation for an exit from this world to the next one God has prepared for us, where Jesus and our loved ones wait for our arrival.

> Imagine if you will that you are sailing on a large ship and you have departed London England's Harbor. You stand on the deck waving good bye to your loved ones who are standing on the docks. They watch as you sail away, and soon they are but a spot in the horizon, but as you turn and look the other direction you can see your

destination and there are some of your
loved ones there waiting for you and they
are shouting and waving at your arrival.[5]

That is what death will be like. One moment you are here, and the next moment you will be in the presence of Jesus escorted by angels. Death is approaching, but you have nothing to fear.

The Frightened Pastor

A pastor who was also a friend and a colleague of mine learned he had terminal cancer. He confided in me about his cancer and put on the most courageous face he could. I was later told by one of his friends that he was afraid of death.

People who are dying will go through moments of fear and doubt and have questions about their faith and God. This is common among the majority of those I have talked too as they were dying.

Among the first questions I ask someone who is close to death are, "Do you have a relationship with God? Is there any unconfessed sin in your life?" This opens the door for them to talk about their fears and doubts, ask questions, or express the fears they might have about death and God and their relationship with Him. This also gives them an opportunity to check their relationship with Jesus, the Savior. Answering these questions and talking about their fears relieves a lot of stress, anxiety, and concern the person might have.

It is also an opportunity for healing not only of a person's relationship with God but also an opportunity to heal relationships with family and friends that need to be healed. These broken relationships will sometimes create more stress in the final moments of a person's life than death itself.

How people approach their deaths can make a big difference with their families as well. If those in the family know their loved ones have a good relationship with God, they're more willing to accept the death of their loved ones, and that will help them with the grieving they need to do.

Some of those who are actively dying may be thinking they have committed some unpardonable sins and it's time for them to reflect on whether they really trust Jesus for their salvation. This gives them the opportunity to take care of that relationship and any questions they have. That relationship is the most important matter that has to be settled as they move toward the end of their lives and death, which waits for them not far down the road.

My friend's cancer was at the stage that nothing could be done to stop its ravaging of his body. He went to the hospital, a place he would never leave. I tried to visit him, but the family said he wasn't having visitors.

As I stood by his door, I could see him and hear him crying in pain and in fear of death. My heart broke for my friend. I could help, but I couldn't get to him with the good news that he didn't have to fear death and that there were angels waiting to escort him to Jesus. Was his fear of death because he had an unforgiven sin in his life and he felt he was beyond any help from God? Perhaps he felt he was beyond hope. I'll never know.

The scriptures are very clear that there is only one unforgivable sin—rejecting of the Holy Spirit. The primary job of the Holy Spirit is to let us know we have broken God's law and been disobedient to God, our Creator. He also lets us know we need to turn to Him and ask forgiveness for our sins, accept the offer of the gift of grace and the sacrifice for our sins, and receive the forgiveness that comes by trusting His Son, Jesus, for our salvation.

As a pastor, I had the blessed privilege of speaking with two World War II veterans who said they couldn't believe God could possibly forgive them for the things they did while they were in the service of their country. Both confessed to me that they had murdered German soldiers during the war. Some people feel they have committed the unpardonable sin, and they have not murdered anyone. They feel they have committed a sin or broken one of God's laws and there is no forgiveness for them.

When this happens, I tell them what I told these veterans. In God's Word is the story of Saul, a persecutor and even killer of Christians in the first century following the death of Christ. Could God, did God, forgive him? Yes. Saul, later named Paul, wrote more books of the Bible than any other writer of scripture.

Paul wrote about many things children of God need

to know about, but the number-one theme of all Paul wrote was about the love and grace of God to forgive our sins. Paul learned as the veterans did that God's grace and love can cover any sin we might commit.

In 1 Peter 2:24, we learn that Jesus bore all our sins—past, present, and future—on the cross. It also tells us we can find the forgiveness we need at the cross. Jesus offers us freedom from the guilt and consequences of our rebellion against God. "He himself bore our sins in his body on the cross, so that we might die to sins and live for righteousness; By his wounds you have been healed" (1 Peter 2:24).

As sinners facing death, we need to make this offer of Jesus for forgiveness our own to deliver us from eternal death and give us eternal life. The Holy Spirit convicts us of our sin and leads us to Jesus, who died so we could have eternal life and the forgiveness of our sins. "But when this perishable will have put on the imperishable, and this mortal will have put on immortality, then will come about the saying that is written: 'Where, O death is your victory? Where, O death is your sting?'" (1 Corinthians 15:54–55).

CHAPTER 2

Angels Are Ministers to Humanity

God loves all humanity. John 3:16 says, "For God so loved the world that he gave his one and only Son, that whoever believes in him shall not perish but have eternal life." And 1 Timothy 2:3–4 says, "This is good, and pleases God our Savior, who wants all people to be saved and to come to knowledge of the truth."

Out of His love for humanity, God sends His angels, His supernatural creations, to minister to us. The Bible uses the word *aggelos*, "messenger," when it refers to angels in the context of supernatural beings that are messengers from God.[1] They were created to be God's instruments or agents to carry out His work. An Associated Press-GfK poll taken in 2011 showed that 77 percent of adults believed in angels.[2]

Let me share again what God's Word says on this subject: "Are not all angels ministering spirits sent to serve those who will inherit salvation?" (Hebrews 1:14).

God's Word is not silent when it comes to the origin, service, and ministry of His messengers and helpers.

Origin of Angels

Angels are beings created by God before the earth was in existence.

Then the LORD spoke to Job out of the storm. He said: "Who is this that obscures my plans with words without knowledge? Brace yourself like a man; I will question you, and you shall answer me. Where were you when I laid the earth's foundation? Tell me, if you understand. Who marked off its dimensions? Surely you know! Who stretched a measuring line across it? On what were its footings set, or who laid its cornerstone – while the morning stars sang together and all the angels shouted for joy?" (Job 38:1-7)

God was telling Job about creation and letting him know that the angels existed before earth did. So the origin of angels is heaven, and they are the creation of God.

Angels are free agents of God committed to do His will. The Bible says, "Praise the Lord, you his angels, you mighty ones who do his bidding, who obey his word" (Psalm 103:20).

Angels have free will and serve Him by choice. Some chose not to serve God; they serve Satan instead.

> And the angels who did not keep their positions of authority but abandoned their proper dwelling – these he has kept in darkness, bound with everlasting chains for judgment on the great Day. (Jude 6)

The Makeup of Angels

I read a story of a child who had a near-death experience. When the child was revived and spoke of the experience, he said he was disappointed the angels she saw didn't have wings.

We often think of angels as having wings and a

human form. The scriptures tell us that angels do take on human form (Genesis 18–19), but there is so much more to angels than that. There is a great difference between humans and angels.

The scriptures tell us we were made a little lower than the angels, yet the Bible tells us that someday we shall judge the angels. In scripture, angels are called "spirits" (Hebrews 1:14). "Are not all angels ministering spirits sent to serve those who will inherit salvation?" (Hebrews 1:14).

Paul wrote in Ephesians 6:12, "For our struggle is not against flesh and blood, but against the rulers, against the authorities, against the powers of this dark world and against the spiritual forces of evil in the heavenly realms."

Angels have supernatural strength. In the book of Acts, we find the disciples freed from prison by angels. It is said, "It was the angels of the Lord that brought down the walls of Jericho." We know they rolled the stone away from Jesus' tomb, and that stone is said to have weighed two tons. The angel that came to free Daniel needed the help of Michael the Archangel. This tells us that the demons of the devil are powerful.

Angels are powerful, but their power does not exceed the power of God.

Isaiah, the Old Testament prophet, described his experience with an angel.

> In the year that King Uzziah died, I saw the LORD, high and exalted, seated on a throne, and the train of his robe filled the temple. Above him were seraphim, each with six wings: with two wings they covered their faces, with two they covered their feet, and with two they were flying. And they were calling to one another: "Holy, holy, holy is the LORD Almighty; the whole earth is full of his glory."
>
> At the sound of their voices the doorposts and thresholds shook and the temple was filled with smoke. "Woe to me!" I cried. "I am ruined! For I am a man of unclean lips, and I live among a people of unclean lips, and my eyes have seen the King, the LORD Almighty."
>
> Then one of the seraphim flew to me with a live coal in his hand, which he had taken with tongs from the altar. With it he touched my mouth and said, "See, this has touched your lips; your guilt is taken away and your sin atoned for." (Isaiah 6:1–7)

Angels cannot be in more than one place at a time, but we are always in their presence. They are powerful beings and can take on human form.

Hebrews 13:1–2 tells us something many don't know: "Keep on loving one another as brothers and sisters. Do not forget to show hospitality to strangers, for by so doing some people have shown hospitality to angels without knowing it."

Angels go before us and prepare our way. They are more than messengers; they have an interest in us. Some say we have at least two angels watching over us at all times. They interact with us when we are not even aware of it.

> Then I asked my master, "What if the woman will not come back with me?" He replied, "The LORD, before whom I have walked faithfully will send his angel with you and make your journey a success, so that you can get a wife for my son from my own clan and from my father's family." (Genesis 24:39–40)

The Protection of the Angels
for God's Children

Notice what God, who cannot lie, tells us about the protection of his children by angels: "The angel of the Lord encamps around those who fear him, and he delivers them" (Psalm 34:7).

God's Word tells us about how angels helped Elisha.

> Then he sent horses and chariots and a strong force there. They went by night and surrounded the city. When the servant of the man of God got up and went out early the next morning, an army with horses and chariots had surrounded the city. 'Oh no, my lord! What shall we do?' the servant asked.
>
> "Don't be afraid," the prophet answered. "Those who are with us are more than those who are with them." And Elisha prayed, "Open his eyes, LORD, so that he may see." Then the LORD opened the servant's eyes, and he looked and saw the hills full of horses and chariots of fire all around Elisha.
>
> As the enemy came down toward him, Elisha prayed to the LORD, "Strike this

army with blindness." So he struck them
with blindness, as Elisha had asked. (2
Kings 6:14–18)

Elisha and his servant saw an army of angels God
had provided for him and his servants' protection.

One of the things we learn from the Bible is that
God uses imperfect men and women to do His will and
work. Abraham was a liar, David committed adultery,
and Paul was a murderer. Peter, the great apostle and
companion of Jesus, denied Jesus three times. Every
one of these examples had angels protecting them.

There is no difference between them and us. Angels
are just as present in our lives as they were in theirs.
We have the same protection they had provided by the
angels of God.

CHAPTER 3

The Man in Stinky Fish

One day, I received a call from my hospice director; he asked if I would go to Stinky Fish to visit a hospice patient who was actively dying. Stinky Fish was a small community not far from where I lived, worked, and served as hospice chaplain. I had been in the community many times before.

I've been frequently asked, "How were you able to deal with all the death, depression, and pain that you saw just about every day?" My answer was clear. "Each time I received a call to visit a dying person, I rejoiced in the Lord because I was being sent by Him to a family that was going through the darkest time any family could go through. If there was the death of a loved one or someone actively dying, I had the blessed privilege of bringing a beacon of light to them and sharing God's love in that time when darkness was the heaviest."

As I pulled into the driveway of the house, a few family members were standing outside dealing as best they could with the situation going on inside. I entered the house and said, "Hello. I'm Richard Burson, the hospice chaplain."

They let me know I was expected. I spoke briefly with the family and let them know I was going to talk frankly and honestly with the man who lay on the hospital bed in the small living room. As I approached him, I could see by his expression that he was concerned about dying, and I knew he had questions about death and dying he needed answered.

I talked to the family about a church relationship and the man's relationship with God and Jesus. I was assured the man had the right relationships with God and Christ. I spoke with him, and he told me his relationship with God was as it should have been because years earlier he had made a profession of faith in Christ as his Lord and Savior.

I sat next to his bed and told him the wonderful

story of how at death the angels would come and carry him into the presence of Jesus. He would see his loved ones who were there and see Jesus. The family members listened intently as I told the Bible story and the promises of God to His children and how death was like the birth of a child.

I spent some time with the man. I left knowing it wouldn't be long before I would get the call that he had died and return to the house to give comfort to his family.

I got that call a few days later. I headed to Stinky Fish again. The family had gathered in the small living room around the bed of their loved one. The wife was weeping, draped over the dead body of the man she loved dearly. She asked me, "Will you tell my children about the angels coming for their dad and taking him home?"

What a blessing it was and is still today to be able to share with people the promise of God that at death, His children will not be alone but will be encircled by angels.

We talked about his life and death. The family told me that a few days before he died, he would look about his surroundings and smile. He would also move his hand around as though he were counting or pointing at something. His final words to his wife came as he rose upon his bed. "The angels have told me that I have to go. I love you." He lay down never to open his eyes again here on this Earth. A moment later, he awoke in heaven.

Cracks in Hell

Jean lived not far from the man in Stinky Fish and was blessed by God because He opened a crack in hell so this precious child He loved would see what awaited her in hell.

The hospice director called me early one morning asking if I could go to the hospital and visit a woman who was dying of cancer.

It wasn't unusual for me to get such calls at any time of the night or day. I always believed I was on call twenty-four hours a day. My wife, Josie, has always been a blessing to me and the ministry God has called me to, and bless her heart, that at times means her waiting up for me to all hours of the night.

The hospital was fairly small. The room was easy to find. It was filled with family members and others who loved the woman. Her name was Jean. She was very active in her church, and church members were there in her room.

I introduced myself and told them I always asked those who were dying if they had a relationship with God and knew God's promises about salvation, forgiveness, and eternal life that came from knowing Jesus as their Savior. The family assured me Jean was a Christian and didn't have to worry about that.

I stood by Jean's bed. We spoke openly and honestly about her coming death. When I asked her about Jesus, forgiveness, and eternal life, she said that she knew Jesus, that I didn't have to be concerned about her. But there was something in our conversation that just didn't seem right. As I left the hospital, I asked myself, *What will happen to this woman when she dies? Where will her soul spend eternity?*

It was a weekday, so I headed to my office and prepared for the day. As I walked across the parking lot, I saw the woman's pastor coming into the hospital. *Probably to see Jean*, I thought. I knew him well. We had done several community events together, and I had breakfast with him about once a week.

I told him I had just visited Jean and asked his permission to continue to see her as the hospice chaplain. He said that would be fine. I asked him if he knew Jean was a Christian. He said, "Yes, she's been a member of my church for many years."

Death doesn't always come quickly to those who are dying. I had expected to get a call within a few days telling me Jean had died. But that would not be the case with Jean; she would live another three months in her private hell.

I stayed in touch through the hospice nurses and visited her occasionally during this time. But each time I visited her, I would walk away with questions in my mind about this woman's very soul. She was a dear, sweet woman who was always gracious, but she never wanted to talk much about her soul and death.

I was expecting a phone call at any time saying that Jean had died. I got a phone call many days later that totally surprised me. The hospice director asked me to go to Jean's house as soon as possible; she said Jean kept screaming at the nurse and the family, "I'm dying and going to hell!"

I got there as fast as I could. The family pointed out her room. When I walked in, she was lying on her bed. Her face was distorted from the crying, shouting, concern, worry, and anguish that was tearing at her soul She looked at me with a horribly distorted face and said in a loud, broken voice, "I am dying and going to hell, I am dying and going to hell, I am dying and going to hell."

"Listen to what God's Word says about this," I said. I told her about God's great love, grace, and mercy He has shown to all humanity. I quoted John 3:16: "For God so loved the world that he gave his one and only Son, that whoever believes in him shall not perish but have eternal life." I explained to her that we were all sinners due to Adam and Eve's disobedience.

I told her that God's Word tells us we have at some time or another disobeyed Him and by doing so would face this very thing she so feared. I told her there was nothing we could do on our own to make ourselves right with God, but God had taken care of that with the death of Jesus on the cross. "He himself bore our sins in his body on the cross, so that we might die to sins and live for righteousness; by his wounds you have been healed" (1 Peter 2:24).

Jean prayed to God, placed her faith in the work of Jesus on the cross that her sins were forgiven, and received eternal life for her soul. I shared with her what happened at death and how the angels would come and escort her to heaven. I could see the peace in her and feel the peace that came into the room that moment as the tears flowed down her cheeks. She received the grace of God in her heart.

I received the call that Jean died just a few days later.

Following the funeral, a family member asked me what had happened in her room that day. The family could hardly believe it. Jean had stopped screaming; she had been more at peace in her final days than at any other time since she had become ill. Though the family members hadn't seen the angels in the room, Jean had constantly told them about them, and she often asked those in the room to move out of her way because she wanted to see the beautiful angels there.

I believe in God's grace and mercy. God loves all He has created and doesn't want any of us to perish. I believe He opened up the gates of hell and let this woman look inside.

God loves us; everyone needs to know that. I wrote this book so others would learn more about the love God has for His children and those who are approaching their final moments on earth.

CHAPTER 4

Angels with Wings

One of the great loves of my life is the hospice nurses who each day bring comfort and compassionate care to hospice patients. They make themselves available all hours of the night and day with hearts filled with love for the people they work with. Every day, hospice patients look forward to visits from their hospice nurses who not only care for them but also for their families.

As I wrote this book, I spoke with hospice nurses who had been caring for patients for many years, and each one tells of events that cannot be explained apart from the supernatural world. Often, as a family listens to the words of the dying, it sounds like babbling. But could it be that the patient is speaking to the angels in his or her room?

The Bus

A hospice nurse told me a story about a man who was in a hospital actively dying. He told those in the room that he needed to get dressed because his bus was coming. His gaze was fixed on a point on the wall. What had attracted all his attention?

Perhaps it was the angels he saw. Perhaps they were telling him it was about time for the trip and a bus would be coming for him. Perhaps he saw the bus that was bound for eternity and he wanted to board it. Whatever it was, it brought him peace.

Going Home

Another hospice nurse told me about a woman who was actively dying in her home and was repeatedly saying to her husband, "I want to go home."

Those gathered around her tried to assure her she was home. The nurse took her husband aside and suggested she may have been thinking of and looking forward to her eternal home. She didn't want to be sick, weak, and helpless any longer.

The husband asked his wife, "Is your eternal home where you want to go?"

A smile came upon the woman's face, and a peace came to her.

Hospital Room 122

The day had begun with a visit to a man who was dying of cancer. As I pulled into the RV park that morning, it wasn't hard to locate where I was to go. The motor home stood out like a bright jewel in a field of cut glass. The size and style of the motor home told me this man had no concerns about money.

Fred was on his way to death's door, and that day, I was about to enter a place of heartbreak, tears, and ultimately rejection. Fred told me to comfort his wife; he told me in so many words, "I don't want to hear any of your spiritual garbage."

When I would visit, a dark cloud hung over any conversation we had. He was pleasant and gracious, but I knew my place and kept it, careful not to cross any boundaries. I always hoped he would want to hear what I wanted to share with him, what God's Word said about Christ, salvation, death, and the angels. His wife, bless her heart, was always so frightened that I would say something that would upset him and take his anger out on her after I left.

His story ended on a sad note. I sat beside the dying man on his deathbed trying one more time just to pray for him. I bent toward him. His voice was weak, and I wanted to hear anything he said. He slapped me. I wasn't bothered by that. I said, "I'm sorry" and left the room. I knew he had slapped me simply because he couldn't slap death. He died cursing me and rejecting the comfort God and the angels would have brought him. He was a very wealthy man who couldn't buy a little peace at his death. How sad.

His story reminds me of the rich man Jesus spoke of in Luke 12. He also had no concern for his soul, for what lay beyond the grave. His focus was on his full barns even though Jesus told him his soul would be required of him that night. He wasn't concerned about rejecting the gift of salvation Jesus offered. (I met many people who had the same response to God's grace toward them; you'll find some of their stories at the end of this book.)

According to the original Greek, Jesus did not say his soul would be required of him but that "His very soul will be ripped from his flesh." There is a ripping and a tearing of the soul from the body. I am reminded of the movie *Ghost* with Demi Moore and Patrick Swayze when the bad guy's soul is taken down to hell by the demons and he has to fight for life and soul. The creatures that sought the man's soul are black, and you just know they're demons from hell. I believe the reason some men and women die in such anger, pain, and fear is because they're fighting to hold onto their lives and because their souls are being ripped from their flesh. They're trying with all their might to hang onto their souls and the things of the world they have stored up.

Luke 12 deals with such a person, but God had a different plan for the man.

> And I'll say to myself, "You have plenty of grain laid up for many years. Take life easy; eat, drink and be merry." But God

said to him, "You fool! This very night
your life will be demanded from you.
Then who will get what you have prepared
for yourself?" (Luke 12:19–20)

After experiences like that of rejection, it was always a task to get my mind back on track to do the things I needed to do. I was looking forward to going home and enjoying being with my Josie, the love of my life. Most nights, she and I sit on the couch—her feet in my lap—and we watch television and enjoy being in love and being together. We have been married for fifty years. That night was no exception.

I got a call from a hospice nurse. A patient's daughter had asked that a hospice chaplain go to the hospital and pray for her mother, who was actively dying and in a coma. She was in room 122 at Mt. View Hospital in Madras.

At that time, I didn't know how significant that information was. I was going on a spiritual adventure that night that would always be in my mind as an epitome experience of God's grace and mercy.

I had never rejected responding to such a call even if they came late at night. I backed out of my driveway that beautiful, starry night and drove to the hospital. I had the code to the back door of the hospital, so there was no need for me to go through the front door and check in. The hallway was dimly lit; faint light came from some of the rooms. I walked the halls to room 122. I heard only the heels of my black penny loafers clicking with each step I took.

The good news and the bad news about this visit was that the woman was in a coma. I thought my prayer would be relatively short and I could get back to my wife and watching TV. The bad news was that I was afraid she wouldn't be able to hear what I said about God, Jesus, and the angels. But I had learned that hearing was the last thing to go when a person was dying, so there was some hope she would be able to hear me. I also knew her spirit was still with her and would hear what I had to say. Not all was hopeless as far as sharing with her what I had to say.

As I came to room 122, I said a short prayer for wisdom and guidance. I quietly knocked on the door. I was surprised when I heard, "Come in." I expected to see a hospice nurse in the room, but I didn't. I saw a woman standing next to the bed. I figured she wasn't a nurse. The hospital gown was a big clue in that regard. I stood for a moment in shock. The patient supposedly in a coma was standing beside her bed wide awake and speaking to me.

"You must be Richard, the hospice chaplain."

"Yes I am." I shook her warm and soft but weak hand. I told her I had come to visit her. "How did you know my name?"

She told me the nurse had told her I was coming. "She left just a moment ago."

I should have seen the nurse as I came up the hallway, but I hadn't. So there I was in room 122 with a woman supposed to be in a coma wide awake and talking to me.

I asked myself, *Do I have a simple prayer with her and call it a night, or should I tell this apparently healthy woman about God, Jesus, and the angels that will come and carry her back to God?* I had been sternly rejected earlier that day by the man in the motorhome, so I was a bit gun-shy about what to do. But then I remembered why I was a hospice chaplain—to help bring peace to those who were dying. With that in mind, I didn't believe I was in that room because of a mistake.

I began to tell her of God's plan of salvation starting with Adam and Eve and ending at the cross with Jesus dying for our sins. I spoke about the forgiveness and eternal life that come with knowing Jesus as our Lord and Savior. I told her that the resurrection was the seal of approval God had put on what Jesus had done. I told her that as a child of God, when she died, the angels would escort her to Jesus in heaven. I prayed with her and left.

I took a different route out of the hospital. I went by the nurses' station. I hesitated at what I was about to ask. I don't like to sound foolish. My question probably sounded weird to the nurses, but I asked them which nurse had been in room 122 earlier.

They were confused. "Why would you ask?" one asked me.

I told them what had happened, and they told me there had not been a nurse in that room since 6:00 p.m. There was no need, they said. The woman in room 122 was in a coma and didn't need the attention; she was expected to die shortly. They said a nurse would go to the room.

I went home that night in wonder and praising

God for His grace and mercy toward this woman. God had awakened her from her coma for a time so I could share with her about the salvation Jesus brings and the angels that come for the children of God at death.

The story did not end when I walked out of the hospital that night. A year and a half later, something happened that confirmed God and an angel had been in room 122 that night. I received confirmation that the nurse who was there that night in room 122 was an angel descended from God.

In central Oregon, there are many pioneer families, and I knew a woman who had lived in the area for close to a hundred years, having moved to that area in the early 1900s as a child. She was a wonderful woman who had many stories that were a joy to listen to. She died at age 104, and I had the privilege of doing her graveside service. It was a simple service in the Pioneer Cemetery. Not many people came; at her age, most of her friends had died and even her family was smaller than most families.

But here's the connection with room 122. After I finished the service, I was visiting with the family and friends when a young woman in her thirties, I'd guess, told me, "You're the hospice chaplain who visited my mother in the hospital."

"I'm sorry, but I can't remember all the people I've visited with."

She told me how she had spent time in prayer for her mother, who had been in room 122 at the hospital in Madras. She told me she had called a hospice nurse late one night to see if the hospice chaplain would visit her mother, who was in a coma. I remembered that night. I asked her how she knew I was the one who had visited with her mother.

She said, "When I prayed, I had a vision and saw an angel in the room with my mother, and then I saw you in that same vision talking to my mother. I recognize you by that spot of gray hair on the back of your head."

I do have that spot of gray, and I then knew the vision had been real; she had indeed seen an angel and me that night in room 122.

I told her that her mother had received Christ as her Lord and Savior and that the angels had come to take her to heaven when she died.

She told me her mother had died that night and, as

far as the nurses knew, her mother had never awakened from her coma. But now we know differently.

She also told me that her mother, prior to that time, had never asked Jesus into her heart. They young woman said she had prayed that somehow, some way, God would send someone to her mother who could share with her about Christ's salvation and that her mother would receive Jesus into her heart. I told her of the miracle that had happened in room 122 that night.

I'm glad I'd gone out that night because I saw God work in a miraculous way that once again showed and proved His love for us and that angels were real and were interacting with us whether we're living or dying.

Someone said that hospice nurses were angels with stethoscopes. That falls way short of describing the hospice nurses I've worked with. They are far more than that to those they treat and love and to their families.

In the years I have served in the pastorate and ministry, I never met anyone who was as loving and kind as the hospice nurses and workers I worked with as a hospice chaplain. I never saw any of them upset at a patient, and they always treated their patients and their patients' families with the highest regard and respect.

We would meet as a hospice team weekly and take a look at the people we would be serving the coming week and speak about the needed treatment and what was going on in their lives. Those closed-door meetings would give the hospice workers a platform on which they could complain and gripe, but I never heard a single complaint from any of the workers. I have seen them give up being with their families to spend the day or night with a dying patient.

An angel had come to room 122 that night as a nurse. But as for me, all hospice nurses are angels with stethoscopes, angels God uses to bring comfort and show His compassion for those who are dying.

Angels in the Room

We've all heard the phrase, "I know I'm preaching to the choir." This is the case with Pastor Collins and me. He was actively dying, and I wanted to share with him the love I had for him. He meant very much not only to me but also to my wife, Josie. I wanted to let him know how much I appreciated all the help in ministry and life that he had given so abundantly to Josie and me. I wanted to remind him about the angels that were to come for him at his death. He was a great man of God and very patient with me. He listened very attentively as I told him about the angels.

I knew he knew these things, but in my zeal to serve the Lord and the blessing that comes from sharing about the angels with the dying, I wanted to tell my pastor about them one more time.

He was lying in a hospital bed in the living room as Josie and I walked into his and Ila Mae's home. Josie and I had been there many times before for dinners, breakfasts, Christmases, and just to visit.

I was intimidated by the idea of sharing about angels with this great man of God, my pastor. I was certain he knew these facts about the angels. I stood beside his bed and saw a man at peace with God, a man who had served the Lord the best he could for many years.

Soon, he would enter heaven through the gates of glory and receive the rewards God promised to all believers. As I began to share with him about the angels that were to come for him, I saw a smile on his face and a glint in his eye. He didn't say a word, but I knew he understood every word I said. I knew he believed and was waiting for the angels to come for him. He would not have to wait very long.

After a very good visit with Pastor and Ila Mae, Josie and I left for central Oregon and the church I pastored and our home. It wasn't many days after we had seen Doyle that he died. I had the blessed privilege of doing the graveside services for this man of God and servant of the most high God.

It has been several years since Doyle died. Not too long ago, I sat in on a Bible study with Ila Mae, Doyle's wife. The subject came up about angels—do we believe in them, what role they play in our lives, and so on. Ila Mae told us of Doyle's death and how in the last few days of his life he had been surrounded by angels. She said that one morning, she saw him motioning with his finger. She asked what he was doing, and he said he was counting. "There are five angels in the room with me. They can move in any direction they want—right or left, up or down—and they can even stand on their heads."

The day passed, the evening came, and Doyle told Ila Mae, "The room is filled with countless angels." Countless angels? Is that possible? Listen to God's Word. God, the Creator of all things, says, "But you have come to Mount Zion, to the city of the living God, the heavenly Jerusalem. You have come to thousands upon thousands of angels in joyful assembly" (Hebrews 12:22).

Billy Graham told the story of his grandmother's death. When she died, her room was filled with a heavenly light. She sat up in bed and almost laughingly said, "I see Jesus. He has his arms outstretched toward me and Ben is with him. [Ben was her husband who had died some years earlier.] And I see the angels." She slumped over, absent from the body but present with the Lord.[1]

Angels are real, and they will be there at death, which is the promise of God to His children: "Precious in the sight of the Lord is the death of his faithful servants" (Psalm 116:15).

Softly and Tenderly

Debbie told a story about a faith-filled woman who was actively dying and in a comatose state. Her family was around her bed sharing wonderful life stories. The patient loved gospel music, so the family was playing some, including,

> Softly and tenderly Jesus is calling,
> calling for you and for me ...
> Come home, come home;
> you who are weary, come home;
> earnestly, tenderly, Jesus is calling,
> calling, O sinner come home![2]

At that moment, this God-fearing woman quietly and gently took her last breath. Then there was a peace on her face that could have come only from the presence of God.

The patient's daughter, son, and I felt a peace that surpassed all understanding. There was a sense that the patient had entered her heavenly home and was in the presence of her heavenly Father and her loved ones already there. The peace never left the room. It's hard to explain the feelings you have when you know and feel the presence of God's angels. There is a peace and an unspoken joy even in this time of loss. There was no doubt in my mind or those in the room that God's angels were in the room.

The Battle Was the Lord's

As my wife, Josie, and I were traveling on the western coast of Washington, we spent a few nights near Aberdeen. At that time, I was doing research for this book. As we traveled and as we had opportunity, we would stop at Goodwill Stores to see if we could find books that would help me.

This particular Goodwill Store had a good section on religion, and I came across several books with information I thought I could use. I knelt down looking at the books and noticed a pair of shoes beside me. I looked up and saw a woman standing next to me. She asked me what I was doing. I told her I was looking for books about angels because I was writing about them and how they were present with the dying and ready to escort them to Jesus. She seemed interested in what I was saying. She told me her story of an encounter with an angel. Her story was interesting; I thought I might use it in this book.

I kept looking through books after she left, but what she had said kept going through my mind. I wanted to hear more about her experience. I found her in the store and introduced myself. She said her name was Willow. She told me more about her experience with the angel. I asked her if I could use her story in my book.

"Yes," she said.

I gave her my email and said I'd contact her.

A few months later, I sent her a questionnaire asking her to describe her encounter with the angel. Here is what she told me.

In April 2012, Willow was diagnosed with cancer. She was told that the doctors had to do some aggressive chemo and radiation treatments. She couldn't believe what she was hearing. She thought the doctors were kidding, but one of them said, "Willow, we don't kid about this."

How could this be? I'm only fifty-two! she thought. She left the hospital and was walking through the parking lot when a tall man with blond hair asked her, "Could you use a hug?"

"Yes," she said.

She allowed him to embrace her. As he was, she sobbed bitterly at the thought of cancer and death. She told him she had only six and a half months to live.

"You will be okay. You will be okay. You will be okay." He said it three times.

Today, the doctors cannot find a trace of the cancer. She lives each day by faith and trust in the Lord and with a peace that surpasses understanding.

She will tell you that on that day in April 2012, she was completely healed by an angel. She will tell you, "Angels are real."

Angels at ninety Miles per Hour

A car was traveling a long stretch of a four-lane highway in Illinois. Music and laughter filled the car as it sped down the highway doing ninety. Three teenagers were in a hurry to get to a bowling alley.

Two cars appeared ahead of them. It was a four-lane

highway, so they were sure there would be room to pass them. The driver jerked the wheel to the left to get into the third lane.

A big truck appeared out of nowhere. No one saw the truck until it was too late. There was no time to react at that speed. As quickly as they changed lanes, they hit the truck head-on at ninety miles an hour. Three teenage boys were at the mercy of all the physics that come with a car traveling so fast and hitting a two-ton truck.

Sitting in the middle was Frank M.; Ed was on his right Frank E. was driving. No one was wearing a seat belt. The boys hit the dashboard on impact with the massive truck. They had little hope of surviving the horrific crash.

Then the strangest thing happened. In just a fraction of a second, the back of the car slid to the right and the passenger door flew open. All three boys were ejected. In the twinkle of an eye, the boys were out of the car and were relatively safe. Ed had suffered a concussion and had to have fifteen stitches, but Frank M. had just a small cut under his chin, as was the case with the driver of the car.

But the story doesn't end there. They were transported by ambulance to a hospital and went into the emergency room to be checked out. All were just thankful to be alive. It was there that Ed began looking at something the others did not see. What was it Ed saw? He said there were three angels in the room with them.

How did that car suddenly turn to the left and the door open, and how was it possible that the three had been ejected rather than crashing through the windshield or being crushed?

If you were to ask them, they would tell you it was the three angels. They saved the lives of those boys that day as they traveled down a highway at ninety miles an hour and hitting a truck head on.

If you asked all three, "Are angels real?" they would have an easy answer. "Yes."

CONCLUSION

This is a book about hope—hope in God's mercy and grace and His eternal ever present love for us as shown in the presence of angels as a person is actively dying. With this book, I want to offer hope to those who face their death or the death of a loved one. This book demonstrates that God holds His hand out to us all and invites us to accept the gift of salvation and the forgiveness of our sins through the sacrifice of His Son, Jesus Christ.

This is a book about the opportunity we have to renew or begin our personal relationship with God. This book is also an encouragement to those who read it to pass this information on to family and friends so they can share with their loved ones that the angels will be with them as they take their last journey through the valley of the shadow of death.

This is a book filled with hope, not condemnation. It is a book for all people who are dying. In the process of dying, people will have doubts and fears; they will be uncertain and have questions. That's all natural and a part of dying. I hope this little book will alleviate some of those fears, doubts, and questions.

Some of those people written about and most of those whose stories aren't in this book had some questions and a certain amount of fear at the thought of dying. But the question is, will you approach those fears, doubts, and questions with hopelessness or with a heart filled with the confidence that God loves you and will send His angels for you?

APPENDIX

"Their Souls Were Ripped from Their Flesh."

And I'll say to myself, "You have plenty of grain laid up for many years. Take life easy; eat, drink and be merry." "But God said to him, 'You fool! This very night your life will be demanded from you. Then who will get what you have prepared for yourself?'" (Luke 12:19–20)

The front of this book is filled with stories of people who in their last few moments of their lives on earth were peaceful, and when they died, the angels came and escorted them to Jesus in heaven.

I've been asked, "Were there some you know who didn't have the same experience?" Yes. I'm not to judge whether a person goes to heaven or hell; that's entirely up to God, the Judge of all. But I can speak from my own experiences, express my own opinions, and draw some conclusions.

As a hospice chaplain, I learned that those who were dying needed reality checks about their relationships with God. I learned that most who are dying have three things on their minds. One is their relationship with God, and they will ask themselves among other things, *Will I be okay and go to heaven when I die, or will God reject me and punish me for the bad things I've done?* The second thing that will be on their minds is *Will my family be okay?* The third is of dying and death: *Will it be painful? What lies beyond the gates of death?*

I couldn't say much about their family situations, but I could speak to the two questions concerning their relationship with God.

I couldn't just barge in and start preaching to the dying, so I would always ask for permission to speak to the patients and their families. Some would say yes and others would say no. I was always respectful of a patient's beliefs no matter what they were.

One of the things important to me as I ministered to hospice patients and talked to them about death, God, angels, heaven, and hell was that if we were to work together in this process of actively dying, we had to be honest with each other. The patient and I would know he or she was dying and there was nothing either of us could do about that. I wasn't there to heal or deal with their physical issues; I was there to help with their spiritual issues and their relationships with God.

As I got to know any one of those to whom I ministered, I would ask, "Do you attend church somewhere? Do you have a pastor I could contact?" Their answers gave me some crucial information about their relationships with God.

If they attended a church, depending on the way they answered the question, I would have a better understanding if they understood or had some understanding of what a relationship with God was all about. If not, I would talk to them about a belief in God. Did they believe in God, the Creator and Judge of humanity?

I would sometimes ask about their family members and if they attended church.

The Soldier

There's always spiritual needs to be met at VA hospitals. Most of those there have experienced bad things and are searching for answers to some of the toughest questions anyone could ask. More often than not, they'll take their doubts, questions, and fears to their graves.

I considered it a great honor to have been asked as a new, young minister to join a team of young ministers and help the chaplain at the VA hospital. One day, the chaplain there asked me to visit a patient. The VA hospital at that time was not the best place to be if you were very sick; they just didn't have the facilities or the personnel and equipment to be better than they were.

The man I was to visit was on the third floor. As I walked upstairs to his room, I kept asking myself what I could say or do that would be best for this man who was dying, possibly without any hope beyond the grave. Then I reminded myself of what the VA chaplain had told me: "All of our hope, whether you are a patient or a minister, is found in Jesus Christ. Our entire future lies in Him who had died for us at Calvary on a cross."

I realized what needed to be done. I entered the room, and the vet was lying on the bed, tubes in arms. The monitor was showing all it needed to show. None of his family was there. The fellow in the next bed was fast asleep. I began with the normal chitchat people engage in during awkward moments. Finally, I got up the courage to ask him about his relationship with God. "Do you attend church somewhere?"

"No."

He said he hadn't been in a church for a very long time. He had planned on going but never did.

I asked him the most important question he may have ever been asked. "If you were to die tonight, do you know for sure you'd go to heaven?"

"No."

"What do you think you would say if you were to die, go to heaven, stand at the gates of heaven, and God asked you, 'Why should I let you into my heaven?'"

"I don't know what I'd say."

"If I could share with you how you could know for sure if you were to die you would go to heaven, would you be interested in hearing it?"

"I would like to hear what you have to say."

I shared with him God's plan of salvation and of his need to repent and to ask God to forgive his sins. I told him he needed to make Jesus the Lord of his life. I asked him if he would like to place his faith in Jesus and know for sure he would get to heaven.

"No," he said. "Not interested in that right now. I'll think about it."

I closed with a word of prayer and left.

The next day when I went to check on him, I learned that he had died just a few minutes after I left, that he had seemed to be in a lot of pain and struggled as he died.

If I knew then what I know now, I would have perhaps been better able to tell him a little more about what lay ahead for him. Perhaps I could have given him a little more hope. The purpose of this book is to bring hope to people like that wonderful vet.

The Walking Man

My pastor was a great man of God who loved the Lord Jesus and sought ways to tell people about their need for Christ. He was my mentor, friend, and pastor. I tried to model my ministry after this great man. If that meant going out in the middle of the night to help someone, that's what I did.

One night, I got a call from a church member. I was asked if I would visit her father, who was in a coma at a hospital.

"Yes I will," I said.

I drove to the hospital. A nurse showed me to the woman's father's room. I knocked on the door.

"Come in."

To my surprise, the man I was to visit was standing by the bed though he was supposed to be on his deathbed and in a coma. I introduced myself, and he responded by telling me his name. I was in the right place with the right person. We talked a little bit about different things, and when I was comfortable, I asked him if he attended a church or had a pastor. He said,

"No, I've never attended church, but my daughter does."

I told him she attended the church I was the pastor of. That seemed to make him relax with me and me with him. I told him his daughter was concerned about his relationship with God, but he said he had no interest in that stuff. I asked him if I could share God's plan of salvation with him. If I could, I told him, I'd be able to tell his daughter I had done at least that.

"Okay," he said.

I spent the next thirty minutes or so telling him how God had sent Jesus to die on the cross for our sins. After telling him the plan of salvation God had for all humanity, I asked if he had changed his mind and would like the assurance in his heart that if he were to die he would go to heaven.

He said he would think about it. He also said he knew he needed to do so.

I prayed and went home.

The next day, I called his daughter and told her what had happened. She told me that the nurse had told her I had visited her father the night before. He had died that night.

In both these cases, I see the grace of God at work in the lives of those He loves. He sends pastors, ministers, and chaplains to visit the sick and the dying because He want all humanity to come to a saving knowledge of Christ. But He will not force people to follow His will for them. He will always give them the choice to follow Him and accept His grace and His love. "There is no reason to die without Christ in your heart."

The Woman in Room 6

As a hospice chaplain, I spent a considerable amount of time visiting patients in senior care facilities. I always enjoyed those visits and listening to their very interesting stories. One woman told me about being left on a snowy mountain while she was pregnant, and I heard from others about how they had made this country great in various ways. They all had one thing in common—they loved to have visitors.

One woman was in room 6 of a senior care facility, and when I went there, I frequently passed her first-floor room. Each time I'd walk by, she would wave and

I'd say, "Hi." I often stopped for a few minutes to visit with this wonderful woman.

She was still in fairly good physical shape for her age, so at times, she'd be out with her family on short trips. Over time, such trips became less frequent, and I'd see her in her room more often.

One day, a nurse told me the woman in room 6 had taken a turn for the worse. I went there and asked if I could talk to her about her relationship with God. She knew who I was, but I'd never gotten into a discussion with her about her beliefs or if she had a relationship with God or even believed in God.

When I asked her, she just about came unglued. She started shouting at me and told me to leave and never come back. I didn't know what I had done, at least not for sure. I suspected it was that any discussion about God was out of the question with her. I immediately left of course. The nurses later told me her family didn't want me to visit with the woman in room 6.

"Okay," I told them. I wasn't about to go against the wishes of the woman, and I wanted to keep a good relationship with the nurses there.

As God would have it, her roommate passed away a

few weeks later and another woman was brought into the room. I had the responsibility to visit with her, so I visited with the new woman but never said a word to the other.

In the following two months, I had the opportunity to tell the woman in the second bed about God's plan of salvation and about the angels that would escort her to Jesus at her death. I didn't know the woman in the first bed was listening.

One day as I passed by room 6, I could see that the woman in the first bed was in trouble; it seemed she was fighting for every breath. I wept for this woman in my heart.

Then the strangest thing happened. She raised her hand, just barely above the edge of the bed, and with her weak hand, she waved me in. She tried to say something. I bent down to hear what she was trying to say. I hoped she wanted me to talk to her about Jesus and the angels. I had a very hard time hearing and understanding what she had to say. I had to have her repeat it three times. I finally understood her. "Tell me about the angels."

I did. I told her about the angels and their coming for her and God's plan of salvation for her.

That day, a woman who had rejected God and the salvation that comes with knowing Jesus as Lord and Savior made a decision that would impact her for eternity. She received a promise from God that when she died, angels would carry her to Jesus because she had accepted the gift God offers through the sacrifice of His Son.

I went back a few more times and just sat and read scripture as I held that precious soul's hand. I would pray, and she would gently squeeze my hand and whisper, "Thank you" with what little breath she had.

The nurses told me that in the final week of her life, she was more at peace than they had ever seen.

God's Word tells us that if Jesus is in our lives, He will give us a peace that will surpass all our abilities to understand. According to God's Word, the woman in room 6 had angels with her in those final days of her life. Peace with God and angels … it doesn't get better than that when we're actively dying as this woman in room 6 found out.

Oftentimes after a person passes away, I will talk to his or her family and explain the difference between a good death and a bad death. Those who have bad deaths have no one around—no family, no friends. They have no peace with God in their hearts or souls. And there are no angels with them in their terrifying moments of death.

Then there's the good death. This is when someone is actively dying but is surrounded by friends and family. They experience the peace of God that surpasses all human understanding and the presence of angels as they surrender their physical beings to death. Their souls leave, escorted to Jesus and the other angels. That is the way all of us should die. That's God's plan for our death.

That is the way the woman in room 6 died—a good death.

The Beauty and Death

One of the saddest and hardest times I had in the years I was a chaplain was when I worked with a woman in her thirties who was dying of cancer. As I write this, my emotions rise and my heart falls thinking about what she went through.

She was married with young children. She was a very beautiful woman; she had a heart and inner beauty you don't often see in a person. Her life and body were being literally torn apart by the enemy of all life, cancer.

Nonetheless, her attitude through all this was one of hope and faith; she trusted in God and had accepted the fact she couldn't change things. Her faith never failed. I never heard her complain once about her pain or the treatments she had undergone. I never heard her ask, "Why, God, is this happening to me?" Such faith is very rare among those who are actively dying.

I suspected I knew where all this came from, but I wanted to be sure. I wanted to know she realized what would happen as she was actively dying. I wanted to know that she was expecting the angels that would be coming for her. As I shared with her, her beauty and her faith came through, and by her expression, I could tell she was listening intently and was understanding everything I was saying.

She was excited as I spoke of Jesus and God's plan of salvation for her. I could tell she had accepted her pending death and was just waiting for the angels to come for her. What a beautiful, good death was coming her way. I missed her after the angels took her to Jesus.

The Perfect Woman

Perceptions, appearances, and what people think are important is the reason we—men and women alike—have so many shops in malls geared toward perceptions and appearances.

If you were to ask them, most people would admit they weren't perfect and didn't know anyone who was. Yet there are people I have worked with as chaplain and pastor who hold some people in such high esteem that it seems to them they can do no wrong.

I met such a woman once. According to her family,

she was the perfect woman. I received a call from hospice; I needed to visit a woman in the hospital who was dying.

I found out the family had a belief system, one I was familiar with but couldn't agree with. However, I was not to judge or condemn any faith anyone held. I would acknowledge people's belief systems and do the best I could to minister to them as a hospice chaplain. I always tried to be polite, never argumentative. My job was to bring hope and peace and do all I could to comfort the patients and the families.

God's Word is very clear—there has never been nor will there ever be a perfect human being. We who are in Jesus will get there someday, but that will be after our deaths. The Word of God tells us this.

> Listen, I tell you a mystery: We will not all sleep, but we will all be changed – in a flash, in the twinkling of an eye, at the last trumpet. For the trumpet will sound, the dead will be raised imperishable, and we will be changed. For the perishable must clothe itself with the imperishable and the mortal with immortality. (1 Corinthians 15:51–53)

The Word of God is clear—Jesus and Jesus alone was perfect while on earth and never committed a sin. He was never disobedient to God the Father, but the rest of us have fallen very short of the mark and standard God has set. In 1 Peter 2:22, we read, "He committed no sin, and no deceit was found in his mouth." And in 1 John 3:5, we read, "But you know that he appeared so that he might take away our sins. And in him is no sin." Jesus said,

> Yet because I tell the truth, you do not believe me! Can any of you prove me guilty of sin? If I am telling the truth, why don't you believe me? He who belongs to God hears what God says. The reason you do not hear is that you do not belong to God. (John 8:45–47)

The hospice director and the nurses were always very careful not to put me in a situation that would be uncomfortable for me, but they couldn't always know the family's belief system.

The hospital set aside a room for those who were actively dying and their families. It was a large room with a television, couch, and a couple of chairs. The hospital would often bring snacks to the family so they wouldn't have to go out for dinner. Time in the respite room varied depending on the patient. Some patients were there for many days while others were there for much shorter times.

In one case, we knew the patient wouldn't be there much more than a week. As I approached, I saw some family members standing by the door of the respite room and in the waiting room outside. I introduced myself and was escorted in by a family member. I was introduced to the family and to the dying woman.

I wasn't aware of the family's belief system. This was early in my hospice ministry, and I had not learned the approach that I would learn and use in the following years.

After the introductions, I asked if I could speak to the woman who was dying. I was somewhat shocked to be asked, "What do you want to talk to her about?" I was under the impression everyone knew what chaplains did, but it certainly wasn't true in this case. I said, "I would like to talk to her about her relationship with God and Jesus."

"What about it? She's a Christian."

"That may be the case, but I would like to talk to her and make sure she knew Jesus died for our sins on the cross."

More than one said, "She's never sinned in her life. She's our mother, and we know she hasn't sinned. You need to leave and not come back."

I excused myself and left, shaking my head. That was an experience I've always carried with me.

GOD'S PLAN OF SALVATION FOR HIS CREATION

God's Word, the Bible, tells us God so loved the world that He gave his only begotten Son, Jesus the Christ, and that whosoever believes and trusts Him for salvation and the forgiveness of sin shall not perish in the lake of fire but shall receive salvation and eternal life. Within that promise is another one that says that when we die as children of God, the angels will come and carry us into heaven.

I hope all who read this book will put their trust for eternal life and the forgiveness of their sins and their souls into the hands of Jesus the Christ, who died on a cross and took all their sins on Himself so this offer from God could be made to all humanity.

EPILOGUE

The Christians who have been martyred for their belief and trust in Jesus and what He did on the cross for everyone are the true heroes of faith. I think God gives them a special blessing and a peace that we ordinary people and Christians cannot understand.

I believe that the angels are there confirming the message of peace and hope that they have in their hearts as they stand before their executers proclaiming the cross and Jesus to all, including their prisoners and executioners. May God bless these martyrs who die for their faith, the cause of Jesus, and as witnesses to us who are watching from afar. Amen.

NOTES

Chapter 1

1 Billy Graham, Dwight L. Moody Quote, *Angels* (Dallas: Word Publishing, 1994), 165.

2 Billy Graham, Charles Spurgeon Quote, *Angels* (Dallas: Word Publishing, 1994), 166.

3 Billy Graham, story about Queen Elizabeth, *Angels* (Dallas: Word Publishing, 1994), 167.

4 Billy Graham, *Angels* (Dallas: Word Publishing, 1994). [No page number]

5 Author unknown.

Chapter 2

1 Judith MacNutt, *Angels Are For Real* (Bloomington, Minnesota: Chosen Books, 2012). [No page number]

2 www.cbsnews.com/news/poll-nearly-8-in-10-americans-believe-in-angels.

Chapter 4

1   Billy Graham, *Angels* (Dallas: Word Publishing, 1994). [No page number]

2   Will L. Thompson, "Softly and Tenderly Jesus Is Calling" (public domain, 1880).

Printed in the United States
By Bookmasters